Withdrawn

DERIAN HATCHER

BOBBY SMITH

JASON ARNOTT

DANNY GRANT

MIKE MODANO

BRETT HULL

LOU NANNE

JOE NIEUWENDYK

DINO CICCARELLI

NEAL BROTEN

SERGEI ZUBOV

BILL GOLDSWORTHY

The History of the

DALLAS
STARS

John Nichols

CREATIVE ☉ EDUCATION

Published by Creative Education, 123 South Broad Street, Mankato, MN 56001

Creative Education is an imprint of The Creative Company.

Designed by Rita Marshall.

Photographs by Hockey Hall of Fame (Graphic Artists, London Life-Portnoy), Icon Sports Media Inc.

(Robert Beck), Sports Gallery Inc. (Al Messerschmidt), SportsChrome USA (Layne Murdoch)

Library of Congress Cataloging-in-Publication Data

Nichols, John, 1966– The history of the Dallas Stars / by John Nichols.

p. cm. — (Stanley Cup champions)   ISBN 1-58341-280-8

Summary: Presents the history, players, and accomplishments of

the Dallas Stars.

1. Dallas Stars (Hockey team)—History—Juvenile literature.

[1. Dallas Stars (Hockey team)—History. 2. Hockey—History.] I. Title. II. Series.

GV848.D35 N53 2003   796.962'64'097642812   2002034932

First Edition 9 8 7 6 5 4 3 2 1

DALLAS IS A CITY WHERE BIGGER IS ALWAYS BETTER.

LOCATED IN NORTH TEXAS, "BIG D," AS IT IS NICK-

NAMED, SERVES AS THE URBAN FOCAL POINT OF THE

state's billion-dollar oil and banking industries. A modern metropolis,

Dallas is known for its big buildings, big money, and passion for

big-time professional sports.

In 1993, Dallas' traditionally football-crazy fans got a new sport

to cheer when the Minnesota North Stars of the National Hockey

League (NHL) relocated to Texas. First hitting the ice in 1967, the

franchise built a winning tradition in Minnesota. But after leaving

the snowy North for the sun-baked South and shortening its name

to the Stars, the team's fortunes skyrocketed. With the support of

their warm-weather fans in the Lone Star State, the Stars have hit

it big in Big D.

BILL MASTERTON

{NORTH STARS ARE BORN} When the NHL decided in 1967 to expand from its original 6 teams to 12, Minnesota was a natural fit. The northern state had long been a hotbed of excellent high school and college hockey. The first North Stars team was a solid one by expansion standards. Led by tough and flamboyant coach and general manager Wren Blair, the team posted a 27–32–15 record. Blair pushed hardworking players such as wing J.P. Parise and goalie Cesare Maniago to excel. "We don't quit," said center Ray Cullen. "Because if you did, you'd have to face Wren."

As promising as that opening season was, it did include a very dark moment. In a game against the Oakland Seals, center Bill Masterton died after being checked to the ice and hitting his head. Masterton, like many players at that time, did not wear a protective helmet. The tragedy eventually led the NHL to make helmet use

Wing Wayne Connelly scored the first two hat tricks (three goals in one game) in club history.

J.P. PARISE

A fan favorite, wing Bill Goldsworthy represented Minnesota in five NHL All-Star Games.

BILL GOLDSWORTHY

mandatory. Masterton is today honored in the form of the Masterton

Trophy, awarded each year to the player who best combines

perseverance, sportsmanship, and dedication to hockey.

The overachieving North Stars made the playoffs

in 1968 and shocked the experts by beating the Los

Angeles Kings in the first round. In the next round,

Minnesota took the St. Louis Blues to a deciding

Cesare Maniago was Minnesota's top goalie in its first nine seasons, posting 29 shutouts.

seventh game but fell 2–1 in overtime. Unfortunately, the North

Stars' surprising first season would be the team's best for the rest of

the 1960s. Sensing that the team needed a change in leadership,

Blair stepped down as coach in 1970.

{GOLDIE SPARKS THE STARS} The North Stars posted their

first winning record in 1971–72, going 37–29–12. One of the big

reasons for the team's surge was the play of the franchise's first

marquee star: wing Bill Goldsworthy. Goldsworthy came to

CESARE MANIAGO

BRETT HULL

Minnesota in 1967 after two uneventful seasons with the Boston

Bruins. In 1969–70, "Goldie," as he came to be known, found his

The **1972–73** | scoring touch, netting 36 goals.

North Stars

won 11

straight   During his 10 seasons in Minnesota, Goldsworthy

games at   led the team in goals six times, including a 48-goal

home, a team   season in 1973–74. He also created a bit of a craze

record that

still stands. | with what fans called the "Goldie Shuffle." After

scoring a goal, the hard-shooting winger would celebrate by doing a

little hop-step while pumping his fist. "Goldie gets the fans worked

up," said Minnesota center Murray Oliver. "And when they get

excited, it helps us play harder."

Goldsworthy had plenty of help in making the North Stars

winners. Fellow wing Danny Grant remained a solid scoring threat

after winning the Calder Trophy as the league's Rookie of the Year in

1968–69. Wing Dennis Hextall, veteran goalie Lorne "Gump" Worsley,

DENNIS HEXTALL

and defenseman Lou Nanne also played key roles in Minnesota's rise.

Goldie, Grant, and company qualified for the postseason four

straight times from 1970 to 1973. Minnesota's best run came in 1971,

when it beat St. Louis in the first round and then played the

Montreal Canadiens tough in the next round before being eliminated.

{MAKING STARS OUT OF BARONS} After being knocked

out of the 1973 playoffs, Minnesota fell into a rut, missing the

playoffs five of the next six seasons. By 1978, the franchise was

sinking fast, and new general manager Lou Nanne was

looking for answers.

Meanwhile, two businessmen named George and

Gordon Gund were dealing with their own faltering

NHL team: the Cleveland Barons. Looking for a way

to reverse their downward spirals, the two teams formed a plan

never before attempted in professional sports—the franchises would

merge. The Gunds bought out the North Stars owners and moved

their best Barons players to Minnesota. With no better options, the

NHL approved the merger. "The league was looking at two franchis-

es in trouble," explained Nanne. "So instead of doing nothing and

maybe losing both, they did what they had to do to keep one alive."

Nanne quickly merged the rosters. The North Stars already

LOU NANNE

featured talented forwards Tim Young and Glen Sharpley. Nanne

then added such Barons standouts as goalie Gilles Meloche and

winger Al MacAdam. In 1978, Nanne also selected high-scoring

center Bobby Smith with Minnesota's top pick in the NHL Draft

and then nabbed center Steve Christoff and defenseman Curt Giles.

Almost overnight, the North Stars were transformed from doormat to Stanley Cup contender. During the 1979–80 season, Minnesota posted a 36–28–16 mark and advanced to the Stanley Cup Semifinals before losing to the Philadelphia Flyers.

{ADDING MUSCLE TO HUSTLE} Hopes were high as Minnesota headed into the 1980–81 season. Head coach Glen Sonmor knew his team had speed and skill, but he felt it lacked toughness. The North Stars played in the Adams Division, home of the rough-and-tumble Boston Bruins and Buffalo Sabres. To strengthen his squad, Sonmor added two tough wings—free agent Jack Carlson and rookie Dino Ciccarelli—to the lineup.

The added muscle paid off in the playoffs when Minnesota out-played and out-hit Boston, Buffalo, and the Calgary Flames on its way to the Stanley Cup Finals. Opposing them in the finals were the defending champion New York Islanders. Minnesota's

A **1980s** standout, center Dave Gagner was a big part of the North Stars' offensive attack.

DAVE GAGNER

From Bobby Smith to Joe Nieuwendyk, the Stars franchise has boasted great centers.

"Cinderella" season came to a close as the Islanders won the series

in five games. "We have nothing to be ashamed of," said goalie Don

Beaupre. "We had lightning in a bottle for a while, but

we just ran out of magic."

The North Stars remained one of the league's top

teams throughout the early '80s. Ciccarelli, Bobby

Smith, and defenseman Craig Hartsburg were all

proven All-Stars. But one player in particular captured the hearts

of Minnesota fans: center Neal Broten.

Broten first found the national spotlight by leading his home-

state University of Minnesota to a national championship in 1979.

The 5-foot-9 and 170-pound speedster then helped the United

States team win the gold medal in the 1980 Olympics. After joining

the North Stars in time for their Stanley Cup run in 1981, Broten

played 16 seasons for the franchise. His career total of 923 points

NEAL BROTEN

(289 goals plus 634 assists) was the second-highest of all time among U.S.-born players at the time of his retirement. "Neal was the guy the fans loved," said center Dave Gagner with a laugh. "I'd

score two goals and the fans would barely cheer. Neal would get one and the place went bananas."

{BACK TO THE FINALS} The North Stars' run of competitive

hockey fizzled out in 1986–87, as the team limped to the first of four straight losing seasons. Ciccarelli posted 52- and 41-goal seasons before being dealt to the Washington Capitals in 1989, but individual performances could not make up for the team's financial problems. In 1990, the Gund brothers sold the team to Canadian businessman Norm Green.

Green and head coach Bob Gainey set about remodeling the North Stars lineup in 1990–91. Young players such as defenseman Mark Tinordi and goalie Jon Casey were given a chance to play and began to improve under the guidance of such veterans as Broten and Gagner. Despite earning a record of only 27–39–14, Minnesota sneaked into the 1991 playoffs.

In the postseason, the scrappy North Stars quickly served notice that they were a force to be reckoned with. Minnesota lost only five games in dispatching Chicago, St. Louis, and Edmonton. Incredibly,

Tough wing Shane Churla spent a team-record 1,883 minutes in the penalty box in the early **'90s**.

SHANE CHURLA

With Jon Casey in goal, the North Stars came within two wins of the Cup in **1991**.

JON CASEY

the North Stars were back in the Stanley Cup Finals.

In the finals, the high-flying North Stars were heavy underdogs to the Pittsburgh Penguins and their star center, Mario Lemieux. Minnesota struck some early blows, winning games one and three, but the Penguins swept the final three games to win the series. "We got this far as a team, and we'll take this loss as a team," said a disappointed Bobby Smith. "It hurts to come so close."

{MOVING TO "BIG D"} The magic generated by the North Stars' amazing 1991 playoff run lasted only a short time. The next two years, Minnesota posted disappointing records. Although the team still drew a lot of fans, most of the local media attention and corporate sponsorship had swung over to the area's newest pro team, the Minnesota Timberwolves of the National Basketball Association. When Green's pleas for help in building a new arena

With a blistering slap shot, wing Dino Ciccarelli averaged 37 goals a season for Minnesota.

DINO CICCARELLI

went unanswered, he decided to move the franchise to Dallas and

rename it the Stars.

The move broke the hearts of many faithful Minnesota fans,

but it created a whirlwind of excitement in Dallas. NHL hockey

had never been played in Texas, and fans there were as curious as

they were enthusiastic. Among the players Dallas fans cheered on were Tinordi, Broten, and rugged defenseman Derian Hatcher. During the 1993–94 season, a new leader also emerged: speedy center Mike Modano.

The 6-foot-3 and 200-pound Modano had broken into the NHL with Minnesota in 1988 and was billed as the league's next great scorer. While he did score, he was criticized at times for being a poor

defensive player. But Modano worked hard and made himself into one of the NHL's best two-way centers, scoring 50 goals in 1993–94 and putting the clamps on opposing teams' top forwards. "Mike could have been happy to be a 30-goal scorer every year, but he knew this team needed him to do more," said Stars center Guy Carbonneau. "To his credit, he took his game to a higher level."

With Modano leading the charge, the Stars began to rise again. In 1997–98, Dallas captured the Central Division title and stormed

GUY CARBONNEAU

into the playoffs. Riding the hot goaltending of veteran Ed Belfour and the clutch scoring of Modano, Dallas beat the San Jose Sharks

Fiery goalie Ed Belfour was one of five Dallas players to play in the **1998** All-Star Game.

and the Edmonton Oilers to earn a berth in the conference finals against the Detroit Red Wings. The Stars battled gamely, but Detroit won in six games.

{CHAMPIONS AT LAST} Before the 1998–99 season, the Stars added a major weapon: free agent wing Brett Hull. One of the league's top scorers for more than a decade, Hull had netted more than 500 goals while playing for Calgary and St. Louis. Hull teamed with Modano, center Joe Nieuwendyk, and defenseman Sergei Zubov to give Dallas a fearsome offensive attack.

Armed with a number of talented scorers, the Stars rolled to a 51–19–12 record. In the 1999 playoffs, Dallas quickly eliminated Edmonton and St. Louis and then downed the Colorado Avalanche in a thrilling seven-game conference finals series.

ED BELFOUR

Facing the Buffalo Sabres in the Stanley Cup Finals, Dallas led

the series 3–2 when the teams met for game six in Buffalo. The game

was a tough defensive struggle, and at the end of

regulation, the score was tied 1–1. The first overtime

went by without a score, as did a second extra session.

But midway through triple-overtime, Hull collected a

loose puck in the Buffalo crease and snapped it into

Wing Jere Lehtinen won the Selke Trophy (as the best defensive wing or center) in **1997–98** and **1998–99**.

the net. After 32 years, the Stars franchise was finally a champion.

"It's an amazing feeling," exclaimed an exhausted Modano.

"Sometimes I wondered if we'd ever get here, but now this city and

this team are finally on top."

The Stars remained one of the NHL's best teams the next two

years, winning their division both seasons. Dallas reached the

Stanley Cup Finals again in 2000 but this time fell to the hard-

hitting New Jersey Devils in six games.

JERE LEHTINEN

Center
Mike Modano
broke virtually
every major
offensive
record in
Stars history.

MIKE MODANO

At 6-foot-5 and 235 pounds, defenseman Derian Hatcher was an imposing figure.

DERIAN HATCHER

Before the 2001–02 season, Hull left town to join the Detroit Red Wings. Then, after the Stars slid down the standings during the

season, the team made a number of personnel moves. Coach Ken Hitchcock and aging standouts such as Belfour and Nieuwendyk departed and were replaced by younger players such as wing Bill Guerin, center Jason Arnott, and goalie Marty Turco.

Folks in Dallas like things big, and for more than three decades, the Stars franchise has been a Texas-sized success. With roots in the wintry North, the franchise has grown tall and strong in the warm sun of the Lone Star State. With the backing of some of the NHL's best fans, it is only a matter of time before these Stars are once again the biggest and brightest in the NHL sky.

BRENDEN MORROW